First Aid
for Cats
The Essential Guide

ROB DUFFY SERIES EDITOR

Published in Great Britain in 2019 by
need2know
Remus House
Coltsfoot Drive
Peterborough
PE2 9BF
Telephone 01733 898103
www.need2knowbooks.co.uk

Contents

Introduction

f you're a cat lover, you'll know there's nothing in the world like it. For those who don't get it, cats seem like lazy, ungrateful animals who wander in and out of your house when they're hungry. Worse, when they get bored, they rip your furniture to bits. These kind of observations usually come from dog owners, or people who prefer their pets docile. To a cat lover, the fact that they do what they want means they're healthy, curious and really alive.

They say curiosity killed the cat. This old phrase, like many, has an element of truth in it. The fact is that cats are curious, and not frightened of what they might discover. Their excellent sight, hearing, smell and whiskers stimulate them into finding out what surrounds them. They patrol the same turf at the same times during the day and night, to make sure nothing untoward has entered their territory. This does, from time to time, inevitably get them into trouble.

One of the many way's cats differ to dogs is that they don't always let you know some thing's wrong. A cat's instinct is to find somewhere quiet to go and lick its wounds or wait until it feels better. You might not know your cat has been in a fight, for instance, until you accidentally stroke a patch of skin which is scratched, bitten or burned. Of course, if you do, your cat is likely to flinch, hiss, attack you and / or run away and hide.

Cats are also prone to certain common ailments. They have their own way of dealing with things they've tried to eat, which may seem alarming at first. Keeping calm when your cat displays behaviour you find alarming is something that many cat owners struggle with. In fact, much of the time, keeping as calm as your cat is the best thing you can do.

When you do discover your cat is in trouble, there are many things you can do which will really help. Once you've learned how to handle your cat when it's distressed, you can make the right choices to get it on the road to recovery. Even if this means getting it to the vet safely, your first aid interventions can be vital.

Being Prepared

f your cat falls ill or suffers injuries of any kind, it may fall to you to treat them. As cats are very self-sufficient, making an intervention will probably be very unusual. Both you and your cat may find the experience somewhat traumatic. While your cat will live its life regardless in the meantime, you should keep at the back of your mind that you may have to help it one day. This preparedness can be as vital as any medical expertise.

Of course, you are not expected to do everything yourself. In most situations, the vet will be the person to properly fix or remedy your cat's injury or illness, however minor. With that in mind, the following should be of comfort in any situation:

A Vet's Obligation

Legally, all veterinary surgeons are obliged to treat any cat, even if it does not belong to their client. All vets must offer an out of hours contact for emergencies. To find a vet in an emergency there are several resources:

Your local listings publications, such as yellow pages;

Any local generic telephone help number, other than the emergency services;

www.any-uk-vet.co.uk

The Royal College of Veterinary Surgeons Website (RCVS)

https://findavet.rcvs.org.uk/home/

Try to always use the number listed instead of one saved in your phone in case the contact number for emergencies has changed. **Always have your vet's number handy.**

> In most situations, the vet will be the person to properly fix or remedy your cat's injury or illness, however minor.

Safety First

It may not always be possible to help your cat. While this might not seem like a positive way to prepare, it should be borne in mind. There may be situations where doing nothing might be the best course of action. It is important to take a breath and consider the consequences of any actions you might take. Rushing in might not be the right way to prove you love your cat.

Think about the following things:

- Will you put your own safety at risk? You are no help to your cat if you yourself get injured, even temporarily. Although cats are resourceful, you are your pet's main source of food and shelter. Ask yourself if there is a likelihood you will suffer injury, say from passing traffic, being swept away by water or even drowning.

- Will your added presence to the situation put your cat or other people at increased risk? Ask yourself whether standing back and offering to help might be a better solution.

- Do you need to call the emergency services? While it might be tempting to think about your cat first, there might be a situation which requires attention immediately. Obvious examples are a road traffic collision, railway accident or burning building. Ask yourself if the emergency services shouldn't be involved as soon as possible.

- Are you ready to take action? Your cat may be in severe pain, which will make it want to strike out and dig its claws into you. You may have to take control of your cat by physical means you would never use otherwise. Ask yourself if you feel ready to overcome your own squeamishness.

By taking these things into consideration, you have already taken the first step in helping your cat, whether he or she is injured or feeling ill. Remember, a cornered cat is not a happy animal. All its instincts will be to get away from its current situation, of which you will be a major part. When it comes to these situations, all bets are off. You may have to overcome the feeling that you are your cat's worst enemy.

First Aid Kit

As being prepared to take the right action is a vital part of giving first aid to your cat, you will find it a great help to have a first aid kit ready. By itemising what is in it, and how to use everything, you should feel more confident if and when the time comes to give first aid. This in turn will help you keep calm and make the right choices. The quicker you take any action, the better.

With a good first aid kit, you will be best placed to take the first steps in getting your cat better. Whether this is just in preparation for a visit to the vet, or a permanent solution, the right tools are a great help. Here are the basics of what you should have at hand, and be confident in using:

- a roll of self-adhesive or crepe bandages (5cm width)
- conforming / open-weave bandages (2.5cm width)
- non-adhesive absorbent dressings (5cm x 5cm) to cover open wounds
- surgical sticky tape
- a box of cotton wool
- a box of sterile absorbent gauze
- blunt ended scissors, preferably curved

- a thick towel
- rectal thermometer
- foil blanket
- disposable, sterile gloves
- saline eye or wound washes
- tweezers
- washing soda crystals
- an Elizabethan collar

An Elizabethan collar has many names, including buster collar, pet cone and E-collar. Light-hearted names include pet lamp-shade and pet radar dish. These collars may look strange, but they prevent your cat from doing what it does naturally – licking its paws to clean its face. As these collars protect the head, this means your cat won't be able to access its own eyes, ears, nose or mouth. If any of these areas is infected or injured, it's vital that they are left alone once treated.

Although your cat will not like wearing one, practice putting one on while it's healthy and contented. This may give you some idea of the challenges you'll face when the time comes to do it for real. Depending on the temperament of your cat, these could be quite considerable. Of course, your cat won't thank you for it, but at least you'll be prepared.

2

What to do in an Emergency

f, after thinking "Safety First" (see Chapter 1), you decide it is safe to make a positive intervention, there are some situations where prompt and effective action can be vital to save your cat.

On no account give your cat any medicine designed for human consumption. If you are taking your cat to the veterinary surgeon, do not give it food or water, in case it might need general anaesthetic.

Describe The Situation Exactly

When calling the vet in an emergency situation, it is essential you think clearly. They will want to know exactly what is happening, and why you called them. Bearing in mind this may not be your usual vet, describing the details of the situation and your cat's symptoms precisely can be life-saving. The vet will want to know:

- What type of problem your cat has, and how severe it is. They will ask if your cat has stopped breathing, or if it has difficulty breathing, how the breaths are coming. The vet will also ask if your cat is bleeding, and if so, how heavily and where from. They might also ask if you suspect your cat has taken poison of some sort, and if so, why you think so.

- How long the problem has been happening. If your cat is showing signs of illness, the vet will want to assess how persistent the illness is. For instance, if it has severe diarrhoea, how often is it, and since when? Also, if you suspect your cat has been poisoned, when was the last time you saw it eat or drink something which might be the cause.

- Exact details about your cat. While some of the vet's questions might seem irrelevant or confusing, they will have good reasons for asking them. Remember, you are talking to the professionals, who will know more about your cat than you do in many ways. Keep a clear head, and remember your cat's breed, sex, weight, age, medical history, any medication it takes and possibly what you feed it. A vet might be able to identify a possible cause of illness very quickly based on their knowledge and experience. This can make treatment much quicker to affect.

Accidents And Severe Onset Illness

If your cat is involved in accidents or mishaps, or becomes trapped in dangerous situations, it will obviously need help as soon as possible. As long as you are in a position to do so, call an emergency vet without delay in the following situations:

- Road traffic accidents, especially when a wheel or wheels goes over any body part

- Penetrating eye or throat injuries

- Impact with your cat's head

- Obvious ingestion of anything toxic

- Overheating or hypothermia.

If your cat is involved in accidents or mishaps, or becomes trapped in dangerous situations, it will obviously need help as soon as possible.

Symptoms Which May Need Quick Action

As cats can be good at hiding their injuries, being vigilant when they come home is always a good idea. Any change in behaviour could signal something is wrong. If your cat usually dashes from the cat flap to its dinner bowl, but doesn't one time, ask yourself why? This will be a natural reaction on your part anyway, so back this up by finding your cat if you can.

Some emergencies affecting your cat are more urgent than others; this doesn't mean they should be given less importance. Of course, heavy bleeding and / or difficulty breathing will be more immediately worrying. Other symptoms may not require immediate attention but remember your cat could be in pain or distress of some kind.

There are other signs which your cat will not be able to hide from you. Have a look out for these:

- Difficulty breathing
- Panting
- Drooling
- Abdominal heaving
- Bleeding
- Foaming at the mouth
- Seizures or muscle spasms
- Persistent vomiting and / or diarrhoea
- Straining when urinating
- Blood in the urine
- Crying when urinating
- Urinating in unusual places
- Licking the urinary area
- Depression
- Lack of appetite
- Lameness
- Weight loss
- Fever
- Dark or bloody stools
- Sunken eyes
- Lethargy
- Dry mouth
- Elevated heart rate
- Decreased skin elasticity
- Squinting
- Pawing the eye / eyes
- Visible third eyelid
- Watery discharge from eye / eyes
- Red, inflamed eyes
- Sticky or yellow eye discharge

If you do have an immediate emergency, it is vital to stay as calm as possible. This will help you keep a clear head, to ask yourself the questions which could lead to a correct diagnosis. If you can't manage this, panicking will only make things worse. Even if you only manage to remember where your vet's number is, any time you save could be of great importance.

3

First Aid Basics
for your Cat

Giving first aid to any living creature is something which benefits from practice. There are physical and emotional barriers to overcome, something which is best done as quickly as possible. If you can, attend a pet first aid course hosted by an accredited pet care organisation. This will give you practical tips based on the experience of other cat owners and veterinary professionals. Unless you've ever given first aid to your cat, or another animal, it's hard to know where to start. This can lead to hesitation and mistakes when action is needed most. Nervousness on your part could do your cat more harm than good.

Familiarity can be extremely important in situations where pain and fear are involved, and especially so with cats. A cat's first instinct when injured or ill may be to attack anything or anyone that comes near it. As a cat owner, hopefully you should have experience of what to expect when approaching your pet. This will guide you as to any precautions you think you should take Always remember, only attempt first aid if you judge it safe to do so.

With that in mind, here are some things to take on board.

Pay Attention

As cats are usually shy creatures, they can be hard to read. Changes in behaviour can be subtle, and very easy to miss if you're not paying attention. What might be easier to spot is erratic behaviour. Cats are often creatures of habit, even if not necessarily at the same time every day. If you notice your cat not doing its usual rounds, for instance, this could be something to watch out for. Cats can suffer from depression or even dehydration, which knocks them off their usual rhythm.

Cats do try to communicate with humans, even if it is not so obvious as with other pets. Your cat will certainly let you know when it's hungry, of course. It will also let you know when it's content, in a number of ways, some of them much subtler then lying on you and purring. For a cat, doing nothing in particular can be a sign that all is well. Doing nothing at all, over a period of days, however, is different. This could be a sign of many a hidden illness, some of which cats are, unfortunately, prone to. We'll see some of them later in this guide.

Of course, the better you know your cat, the easier the signs will be to spot that something is wrong. It may just be a tick, for example, which is easily removed if you have your tick remover with you. The point is, the sooner you spot any danger signs, the better position you are in to do something about it.

> As cats are usually shy creatures, they can be hard to read. Changes in behaviour can be subtle, and very easy to miss if you're not paying attention.

Call the Vet First

Before you take any action yourself, call your vet. Even if your usual vet is not there in person, someone will be able to assist you. Don't act without asking advice first. Your veterinary surgery may advise you not to do anything and wait for someone to come to you. Alternatively, they may advise you to take your cat to them yourself, if you have suitable means of doing so safely.

Calming and Preparing Your Cat

If your cat has suffered a distressing injury, or is feeling particularly unwell, you may need to stabilise it. As cats are very sensitive creatures, they can become upset easily. This can lead to further injury or worse illness, as the cat panics because of something it doesn't understand.

Even if you are able to deal with the problem yourself, you will find that having techniques to calm and stabilise your cat come in extremely useful. If, on the other hand, you need to wait for, or travel to, a vet, keeping your cat stable can be absolutely vital to its overall health and well-being.

1 **Protection.** Wear long sleeved and legged clothing. Your cat may try to bite and or scratch you. Also, carry a thick towel, in case you need to grab your pet. Approach with extreme caution, slowly and deliberately.

2 **Preparation.** Calm your cat using any and all methods you can think of. Normality is calming, for instance; put the television or radio on, as you would normally. Sing softly, especially if this is something you normally do around your cat. Talk to it calmly, letting it know every thing's all right. Sit down and be patient.

3 **Enticement.** Once your cat is somewhat calmer, offer it some food. As cats prefer wet food rather than dry, open some of this. If you have some fishy food handy, use that. Cats love the smell of fish, which takes their mind off just about everything else that's going on. Once your cat accepts the food, stroke it gently with your thumb, from its nose upwards.

4 **Isolation.** If none of the above calms your cat to a point where you can approach it, the best thing will be to isolate it. This will be its natural instinct anyway, so it will cooperate with you if you help it work with you.

You can do this by leaving it in the room it's already in, and removing distractions one by one. Get everyone out of the room, turn everything off, and close the curtains. Then back out of the room and close the door.

If you want to take your cat into another room, you should do this carefully. Find and prepare a small room first, which is quiet and dark. Approach your cat as detailed above, using your towel, pick it up and cradle it so just its head is visible. Talking to it calmly, carry it into the quiet room, lay it down and back out, closing the door behind you.

Once your cat is safely calmed down, and depending on the situation as outlined above, you may be able to apply first aid yourself, if your vet has advised it. Otherwise, your cat is able to be calmly transported to the veterinary surgery.

Spray your cat's carrier with a synthetic pheromone cat scent, at least 15 minutes before using it. If you know that your cat will panic when it sees the carrier, put it close by, but out of sight.

Choking and Resuscitation

4

Choking

hoking is one of the most worrying things that can happen to your cat. It will be extremely distressed and frightened, and no doubt so will you. It is, of course, vital not to panic in such a situation. You will need a very calm head in order to act quickly to remove the obstacle. Depending on how long the choking has been happening, you might then need to resuscitate your cat. Both of these steps can be achieved with the right knowledge and attitude on your behalf.

If your cat is showing signs of choking, you will first need to restrain it. As it will already be in a state of panic, any attempt on your part to access its throat will cause it to want to bite you. In other situations, your cat might actually be unconscious. If this is the case, the procedure is slightly different.

What to Look Out For

If your cat is choking, it has something stuck in its larynx or trachea. If this is the case, these are the signs to look for:

- Anxiety or panic
- Bad breath, loss of appetite, or listlessness
- Coughing or gagging
- Fainting, unconsciousness, or inability to breathe
- Laboured breathing
- Pawing at the mouth, and / or drooling.

Gaining Access

If you have calmed and restrained your cat, or if it is unconscious, its mouth may be shut. To open it, take hold of its upper jaw with your fingers and thumb. This is the safest way of ensuring your cat is not able to bite you, whether it is conscious or not. If it is unconscious and wakes up suddenly, its first instinct may well be to bite.

- Open your cat's mouth fully with your other hand. Pull its tongue forward and down, and have a look deep into the back of its mouth. If you can see what is causing the blockage.

- If you can see an object in your cat's throat, take the tweezers from the first aid kid and try to take hold of it. If you get a decent grip, try to pull it forwards out of your cat's mouth.

- If the obstruction is a piece of bone, this is hard to do. Don't spend too long trying to remove any object if you can't get a decent grip. It's more important to take your cat to the vet's as soon as possible.

If you can't see any obstruction, your next step should be the Heimlich Manoeuvre. This is something you should practice on a Pet First Aid course as soon as you get the chance.

- Lie your cat on its side. Put the flat of one hand along the length of its back.

- Place the flat of your other hand on your cat's abdomen, just below the ribcage. Put the heel of your hand furthest away from its head, with your fingers facing that way.

- With one hand steady against your cat's spine, push the heel of your other hand sharply into its belly, below the ribs. Do this a few times, quickly.

- Check your cat's mouth, to see if there are any foreign objects in it which have been dislodged by your attempts. If there is anything there, pull it away.

- Close your cat's mouth and breathe into its nose a couple of times.

- Repeat this whole process until you are sure there is nothing left obstructing your cat's throat.

- If you cannot dislodge the choking object from your cat's throat, take it to a vet immediately. See our section on *Transporting Your Cat Safely*.

If you do manage to dislodge the object, your cat may start breathing again spontaneously. If it does not, you'll need to resuscitate it.

Acting quickly and appropriately in the right circumstances can quite simply save your cat's life.

Resuscitation

One of the most important things you may ever be able to do for your cat is resuscitate it. While this process is something mostly associated with people, in fact it is perfectly possible to carry out on your pet. Acting quickly and appropriately in the right circumstances can quite simply save your cat's life. Of course, no cat owner ever wants to be put in such a situation. If you are, however, it is helpful to remember that the successful steps to resuscitation are literally A, B, C. This stands for Airway, Breathing and Circulation.

ABC and CPR

Another handy acronym to remember when thinking about resuscitating your cat is CPR. This stands for Cardio Pulmonary Resuscitation and works on exactly the same principles as with humans. Basically, if your cat is in serious trouble and has stopped breathing, you can resuscitate it by getting its heart and lungs working properly again. The quicker you are able to do this, as with humans, the less damage is likely to have been done. As long as your pet's brain has not been starved of oxygen for too long, a complete recovery is possible.

Of course, you need to be confident when attempting CPR on your cat. There are classes available which will show you what to look for, and what procedures to carry out. These use feline CPR manikins, which are specially designed to give you an idea of what it feels like to resuscitate your cat.

What manikins cannot replicate, however, is the smell of your cat's breath. Like the shape of its whiskers, you will no doubt be familiar with this. It is details such as these which can tell you if your cat is need of resuscitation.

Airway

If your cat is immobile and you cannot rouse it, there is obviously something wrong. In order to check to see if it's breathing, you can look for its ribcage. If you feel or see no movement there, check its nose. You will be able to see any signs of breath on its whiskers. If these are still, put your face close to your cat's mouth and nose. You will be able to detect the smell of its breath if it is breathing.

If none of these signs are present, open your cat's mouth gently. Pull its tongue forward out of the way and check inside for any objects in its throat. If you see something, try and remove it with tweezers. Do not push any obstructions further down your cat's throat. Pull the tongue all the way out in order to help any object free itself.

Once any obstructions are out of the way, your cat may start to breathe. If it does not, and you are sure there are no obstructions in its throat, you should check for a heartbeat. To do this, put your finger tips under your cat's left leg where it joins its body. You will feel any heart beat through gaps in its ribs. If you feel nothing, you need to start resuscitation quickly.

Breathing

With your cat on its side, lift its nose upwards slightly so that its head tilts backward enough to open its airway completely. Once you've done this, pull your cat's tongue to the front of its mouth, just behind its teeth. With the tongue in that position, gently close your cat's mouth, and hold it shut.

- Making sure your cat's neck is straight, in line with its spine, breath into your cat's nose, once every four to five seconds. As you'll have your lips pursed, you won't be able to blow too much air into your cat's lungs, so don't worry about that. Do this three to five times, then check your cat for a heartbeat and / or breathing.

- If there is still no sign of either, repeat the above, with one breath every six seconds, or ten a minute. You will need someone to drive you and your cat to the vet while you are doing this.

Circulation

If your cat's heart stops, you will need to get it started again. To help get your cat's heart beating, combine breathing with compression. In between breaths, compress your cat's ribcage enough to press on its heart.

- Lay your cat on its side, preferably on a hard, flat surface. This should also be far enough from the ground to give you reasonable access to it without bending all the way down every time. This treatment may last quite a long time.

- Using just one hand, put your thumb on one side, and fingers on the other, of its ribcage. You should do this just behind your cat's elbows, where its front legs join its body.

- Squeeze quickly, to a degree just enough to compress your cat's chest to about half its normal capacity.

- Try to get into a rhythm between breathing and compression. You want to compress your cat's chest 15 times every ten seconds. In the meantime, try to breathe into your cat's nose after every 10 compressions.

Checking for Signs

After a minute, re check your cat for signs of breathing and heartbeat. It is possible that it has started breathing while you were administering CPR. If not, repeat the process 10 times, over 10 minutes. If there is no sign of breathing after this, unfortunately it is unlikely to return.

If you are successful in resuscitating your cat, remember to take it to the veterinary surgery as soon as possible. For help in doing this, see the next chapter of our guide, *Transporting Your Cat Safely*.

At the Vet's

Once you've reached the veterinary surgery, the vet on duty will examine your cat before they take any further steps. They will assess the condition of your cat's heart and lungs, to see if they should proceed with their own resuscitation efforts. Be prepared for this, as the vet may decide you have done all that could be done.

If they do proceed with further resuscitation, and revive your cat, they will then carry out further tests to see if there are any underlying health problems. If you have taken resuscitation steps because your cat was choking, you might find this confusing. In fact, this is the perfect time to find out if your cat is otherwise healthy.

Your vet's CPR treatment will be different to that of your own first aid efforts. As they are the experts, and have all the latest equipment, this is only to be expected. The following are standard procedures in veterinary surgeries:

- Endotracheal Tube. This is a much more efficient means of getting air into your cat's body than blowing through its nose. The tube delivers oxygen directly to the lungs, via your cat's trachea.

- Intravenous Catheter. This very minor procedure allows easier administration of emergency medication and can be used to rehydrate your cat.

- Epinephrine is a powerful drug, delivered through the intravenous catheter, which stimulates both your cat's heart and its breathing.

Warning: Unfortunately, the nature of a cat's cardiovascular system means that, if CPR becomes necessary, your cat is unlikely to survive. If it does, it will be very ill for some time. Your vet will keep your cat in hospital conditions, until they are satisfied that all tests have been completed. The financial implications of all of this will be broached by your vet, which is something you need to be prepared for.

5

Transporting Your Cat Safely

Applying first aid to your cat is an excellent first step in ensuring its full recovery from illness or injury. In many cases, however, it is just that; a first step. Most of the time, as you will read in this guide, the first aid treatment is completed by a trip to the veterinary surgery. Just as you wouldn't trust yourself to cure your family of many of the ailments described here, so you should entrust the health of your cat to the professionals.

In fact, transporting your cat safely is an excellent first aid skill to have generally. You may need to take your cat to many places, not just to the vet. Cats are designed to prowl and roam free, not sit in cages looking out of windows. For this reason, they can become distressed when forced into such a situation. While you know it's for their own good, they don't.

Learning how to get your cat safely from a to b while not under its own devices could serve both you and it well in the future.

The Right Carrier

Being transported in a vehicle is one of the least likely things a cat was ever designed for. Being curious, self-reliant creatures, they will naturally wonder what is going on every second of the way. This may be helped by them not feeling well, but on the other hand, that could make the situation worse. If your cat is distressed, any extra stress will add to its anxiety. Having a cat carrier which your pet is used to will make taking it to the vet or anywhere else much, much easier.

As there is an ever growing range of cat carriers to choose from, here are essentials to help you choose the right one for you and your pet:

1 Quality. As cats are strong, wilful animals with sharp teeth and claws, your cat carrier will have to be well made. This means having a mesh your cat can't break through, as well as nothing it can harm itself on in the interior. You will also need a carrier with excellent seams, be they stitched, zipped of held with Velcro. Remember, you are carrying both a carrier and your cat at the same time. If your pet is on the large side, you won't have the luxury of cradling it in your arms as usual.

2 Size. Your carrier is not a cage, even though it will have grilles. Your cat needs to have enough room to move freely, even if it can't. Remember, cats need their space, wherever they are.

> Learning how to get your cat safely from a to b while not under its own steam could serve both you and it well in the future.

3 **Handles and Shoulder Straps.** Taking control of a cat in its carrier is not always easy. Even a shopping bag with similar weight wouldn't be the easiest thing to carry. Bearing in mind you have a sick, living animal in what is essentially a box with you, it's best to have all the tools necessary. Manoeuvring from your home to your vehicle, then out again into the veterinary surgery, takes some consideration. Think about how far your vehicle is from your home, and also where you are likely to be able to park at the other end. Carrying equipment such as handles, and straps should be of the highest quality.

Getting Acquainted

So that your cat is as comfortable as possible when being transported, it should be well used to its carrier. Getting inside it should be as much as possible part of your pet's normal routine. This avoids adding stress to a first aid or emergency situation.

Ideally, your cat should see the carrier as part of its home. Keep it in the same place, as part of the furniture. Have it open at all times, so your cat can explore it like it would anywhere else. It may well choose to spend time there at certain times of the day.

You could also put a blanket in there, and maybe some toys. You may find that it puts its own favourites in there of its own accord. This is a sign that your cat is comfortable being in its carrier. Remember, cats have a superb sense of smell, and will detect foreign objects immediately. Anything connected with your pet's carrier should be familiar to it, so its senses don't react adversely when the time comes to use the carrier.

In Transit

When actually taking your cat anywhere in its carrier, try to make the experience as stress free as possible. Make sure your pet is comfortable inside the carrier, whether it needs protection with a towel, or can move more freely. When you get your cat and carrier into your vehicle, make sure you leave it there. Don't be tempted to let your cat out of its carrier to have a bit more room. Even on non-essential journeys, this is a bad idea. Just because there is more room inside your vehicle, doesn't mean you should let your cat explore it.

When you have the carrier in place, secure it properly. Whether this is in the back seat, or you have a hatchback or bigger area, use the appropriate belts and anchor points. Some modern vehicles come with specially designed harnesses and / or belts which will accommodate a cat carrier.

- **Do not** place your carrier in a closed trunk of any kind. If you have a vehicle with carrying facilities for other purposes, don't be tempted to put your cat and carrier in there. Cats will panic in a dark, moving box, however short the journey. This could seriously compromise their health, especially when they are already ill and distressed.

- **Remember air bags.** If you have to put your cat carrier in the front passenger seat, remember to disable the air bag on that side. As air bags can activate very quickly in all sorts of circumstances, don't take the risk of your passenger air bag doing this while your poorly cat is in its carrier. Your cat could be injured by being thrown around inside its carrier, and certainly won't feel any better for the experience.

Bandaging and Medication

Learning how to apply bandages to your cat can be a superb first aid skill. Bandaging can help support damaged limbs as well as holding dressings in place. A properly applied bandage will help your cat feel safe while its wounds heal. Similarly, learning how to give your cat medication is something that not everyone knows how to do properly, but is an important procedure. As there could be a whole host of reasons why your cat needs to take medication, and they don't like taking it, knowing how to do this safely is an excellent first aid skill.

Principles of Bandaging

Of course, veterinary nurses are the experts at applying bandages, and you should take your cat to the veterinary surgery for real professional bandaging but following the right steps can really help your cat in the meantime. On the other hand, a badly applied bandage can actually do your cat harm.

It is recognised best practice for bandaging to consist of four layers;

- A non adhesive dressing directly touching the skin. This is especially important in the case of bleeds and burns and is known as the swab layer. This layer must be absolutely sterile and sit on skin which has been thoroughly cleaned.

- On top of the swab layer, a conforming cotton wool bandage is applied to completely cover the swab and surrounding area.

- The third layer is conforming bandage, which holds the first two firmly in place against the skin.

- Finally, an outer layer of vetwrap or other brand of non-adhesive material completes the bandaging.

Depending on the type of injury your cat has, once bandaging is in place it may be left for varying lengths of time. Open wounds and burns will require bandaging to be checked and changed once a day. This is both to see how the wound is progressing, and to check for any signs of infection. Bandaging which is used to support limbs after sprains etc. can be left in place for longer periods. Your vet will advise you when to come in for a change; this itself can change if the bandaging comes loose, wet, damaged or your cat chews it.

In the case of your cat's leg, a veterinary nurse will bandage the whole limb. This might seem strange at first, but there are excellent reasons for it. No matter where the wound is, or whether it is internal or external, bandaging needs to be done properly. This is mainly due to blood supply.

- A properly applied bandage will always start from below the wound; this means as far away from the heart as possible.

When applying a bandage, you should bear this in mind. You don't want to wrap bandages too tightly, but they have to be tight enough to keep the layers in place. By starting after the wound, it's easier to judge tension, and it avoids the danger of cutting off blood supply before it gets to the affected area. Working inwards is the best way of ensuring continued blood supply.

If your cat has a bandaged limb, there are ways of checking to see if its blood supply is still healthy. If it is not, you could notice one or more of the following signs:

- A swollen paw or distal limb
- Red or purple skin beyond the bandaged area
- Cold feeling paws or lower legs
- A foul smell coming from the wound
- Your cat repeatedly trying to lick and or chew its wound.

Your cat needs its blood supply to heal its injury, whether that is a bleed, burn, break or sprain. Apart from this basic requirement, bandages wrapped too tightly will be uncomfortable, and may cause numbness. If you notice your cat in any distress after bandaging, inform your vet straight away. When applying bandages, yourself, try not to wrap the outer layer too tightly. This is especially important if you are not planning to take your cat to the vet, perhaps because it only has a minor injury. Be careful not to assume that your cat is showing signs of distress purely because of its injury. It could be trying to tell you that its bandages are too tight.

A properly applied bandage will always start from below the wound; this means as far away from the heart as possible.

Medication

When administering medicine to your cat, you need to be prepared. Doses and medications for cats are very precise and need to be delivered as such. Missing one, or giving too much, could be very damaging to your cat's health. Combine this with your cat's innate opposition to having anything administered to it whatsoever, and you have an idea of what you face.

Because cats are suspicious of things they don't like, cat medicine has been developed into various guises. Powders and liquids are favourite, because they can be disguised. All the same, when giving your cat any kind of medicine, it's best to do it in private.

- **Avoid distractions** like children, and other pets, when the time comes to give your cat its medication.

After taking this simple precaution, there are two ways to make giving your cat its medicine as easy as possible. Bear in mind that your cat may bite you if you try to force it to take something it doesn't want to.

Mixing With Food

This is a favourite method among cat owners trying to make sure their pet gets the medication it needs. The idea is that your cat won't notice there is something in its usual food which shouldn't be there. Of course, your cat has an array of senses you literally can't imagine, so getting this right takes some thought.

- Your vet will advise you whether your cat's medication is suitable to be mixed with food. If you are in any doubt, read the label carefully. Have all your ducks in a row before you try to give your cat its medication, as you may only have one chance. Be sure you know the right dosage and frequency before you start.

- If you have to grind tablets, don't lose any of the medication in them. Use a pestle and mortar if you have them, or make sure you have a smooth surface to catch any granules if you are using the back of a spoon. Pill crushers are available, which may be best for long term medication.

- Make sure your cat is hungry before you administer its medication. This will give you the best chance of delivery, as your pet will do the work for you. Leave at least 6 hours before serving your cat's food, however much it pleads. Delivering medication means being strong. Remember, if your cat leaves some of its food, it won't be getting all the medication it needs.

- Use wet food, such as meat or fish (fish is especially good) and stir the medication in well. Leave it for at least 5 minutes, so any taste has been absorbed by the food.

- You might want to try this **trick**; Have the ready mixed medicine and food ready, hidden from your cat's view, on the bench in front of you. Then, make like you're reaching for your cat's favourite food, from the cupboard you always keep it. Go through your usual routine and reach toward your cat's favourite bowl. Then, turn back around, and get the food / medicine mixture you've already prepared. Put this in the bowl, by which time your cat will be just about ready to eat your hand. Hopefully, between this and the medicine being fully absorbed into the food mixture, your cat will devour everything in its bowl.

- Don't watch your cat eating, unless you usually do. Just act normal, until your pet has finished its meal.

Once you're sure it's finished, and preferably your cat is out of the way, check the bowl to make sure it's been licked clean. Cats will simply separate out fragments of anything they don't want to eat, if they can.

Using Pill Poppers

Some medication for cats isn't made to be digested, therefore should not be eaten. This comes in the form of enteric-coated capsules. The coating is there to resist the acids in your cat's stomach, so the capsule can pass unharmed into the gut itself. To administer this type of medication to your cat, you will need what is commonly known as a pill popper. Although this is not strictly necessary, using one of these devices means your cat will get is medication, and you won't get bit. Bearing in mind you are trying to force something into your cat's mouth, this is highly likely.

- If you have a particularly nervous cat, you may want to swaddle it in a thick towel before you use this form of administration. In any case, this is what to do:

- Put the correct dose of medication in the device, ready for use. Put the popper in front of your cat, on a suitable surface, so it doesn't come as a surprise.

- Position yourself and your cat so that you can gain access to its medication, talk to your pet and administer the dose at the same time. The best way to do this is by having your cat on the opposite side of your body to the hand you will use. Your cat should be facing you, with its hind quarters against something so it can't wriggle away. If you have someone to help you, they can do this without causing your cat any stress.

- Take hold of your cat's head, gently but firmly, with your free hand. Raise your pet's face to the ceiling, lifting its head at the same time. This will make your cat reach forward with its front legs and open its mouth to breathe better. Make sure you keep your hands and arms out of the range of your cat's claws, in case it lashes out.

- Put the pill popper inside your cat's mouth, as far back as you can, right in the middle of the tongue. Release the capsule, and with the implement still in place, start closing your cat's mouth around it, and pull it out.

- Once the pill popper is out of your cat's mouth, keep your cat's mouth closed and gently tilt its head and face downwards. The combined effect of the pill falling backwards and its mouth closing will make your cat swallow the capsule automatically.

- While you still have control of your cat's head, you could try gently massaging its neck to stimulate the swallowing reflex. Also, injecting water into the side of its mouth with a syringe will encourage its natural swallowing reflex.

- Gently release your hold of your cat's head and see if it licks its lips and / or nose. This means it has swallowed the capsule.

- If your cat spits the capsule out, you will have to try again. If it is distressed, wait a while until it calms down; otherwise, as you have your pet in a good position, it is best to try again immediately. Remember to stay calm, and don't utter any negative sounds.

7

Dealing with Bleeding

After resuscitation, one of the major ways you can help your cat with first aid is by dealing with bleeding. While this can be traumatic for both your pet and you, it is an excellent set of skills to have. Apart from your cat not breathing, nothing signals that its health is in danger than the loss of blood. Although major bleeds are more obviously upsetting initially, even minor ones can be serious if not treated promptly and correctly.

If you are frightened by the sight of blood, it's a good idea to find ways of getting over this. Cats can bleed for all sorts of reasons. Also, cats usually have dense fur which soaks up blood. You may have to get to the source of the bleeding to determine what if anything you should do about it. The braver you can be, the better the result for your cat, both in the short term and the long run.

External Bleeding

Apart from the likely distress it will cause, the main reason to stop bleeding as soon as possible is to prevent shock. If your cat loses enough blood, its nervous system will go into shock, which can be extremely serious. If your cat has pale or white gums, is breathing rapidly, or you can see or feel its heart beating very quickly, it could be in shock. By staunching bleeding quickly, this can be avoided.

As with cuts to human skin, a quick way to stop bleeding is to apply pressure. Of course, this will be easier to achieve on some parts of your cat than others. If your cat is actually spouting blood, it will need professional help immediately. For most types of external bleed, however, first aid is quite straightforward to administer.

(For the sake of convenience, we'll assume you are at home and have access to your cat's first aid kit. If you are out and about, you may be able to improvise, or you may decide it's best to call the vet and ask their advice.)

Bleeding from the Head or Torso

To treat bleeding from your cat's head or torso, you will first have to restrain it. The idea is to immobilise your cat's head completely. This will keep you safe and stop the cat from further injuring itself.

Once you have your cat's head immobilised, you can safely treat the source of your cat's bleeding, as follows:

Apart from the likely distress it will cause, the main reason to stop bleeding as soon as possible is to prevent shock.

1 Apply pressure directly to the wound. It should stop bleeding after no more than a couple of minutes.

2 Once bleeding is staunched, cover the wound with fresh gauze pad, clean towel or appropriate sanitary material.

3 Wrap the dressing with soft cloths or other bandage material (see *Principles of Bandaging*), just tight enough to keep the dressing in place.

4 Take your cat carefully to the vet (see *Transporting Your Cat Safely*).

Bleeding Leg, Paw or Tail

Bleeding from any of these appendages will inevitably cause your cat to lick the affected area, and probably cry. Again, you'll need to restrain your cat safely, using a reassuring voice. Once your cat is calm enough to work with, take the following steps:

1 Clip the hair around the affected area carefully to gain access to the wound.

2 Examine the wound for any objects still in it. This could often be glass, so be careful not to cut yourself or further injure your cat. If you can see a foreign object, remove it as gently as possible with tweezers or your fingers if necessary.

3 Move the skin gently backwards and forwards around the wound. If the wound does not completely move with the skin, it will be deep enough to need stitches.

4 Flush the wound out using clean water. Do not apply any antiseptics, as these will be painful for your cat and distress it further. You want your cat as calm as possible while you are applying first aid.

5 Cover the wound with a new gauze pad or another sterile dressing.

6 Put your hand all the way over the dressing and press down firmly.

7 Keep applying pressure to try to stop the bleeding. If blood soaks through the dressing, **do not** remove it, but add another dressing and continue applying pressure. After 5 minutes, if the bleeding has not stopped, you'll need to go to the veterinary surgery immediately, or call out an emergency vet if you can. In the meantime, keep applying pressure to the wound and adding extra dressings if needed.

8 If only a couple of specks of blood are visible through the top layer of dressing, you have successfully staunched the bleeding. Well done! Now, keep the dressings in place and wrap them with bandage material (see *Principles of Bandaging*). Start beyond the wound and wrap inwards, don't wind the bandage too tight, and tape in place when you're finished.

9 If you saw that the wound needed stitching, take your cat to the vet and keep it off its injured leg on the way (see *Transporting Your Cat Safely*).

Bleeding Chest or Abdomen

A wound in either of these areas means you will have to restrain your cat safely. Once you have done this, examine your cat either on its side, sitting or standing depending where the bleeding is coming from.

1 If the bleeding is coming from the chest area around the rib cage, listen carefully. If you can hear a sucking sound, you need to get your cat to a vet as soon as possible. Put bandaging around your cat over the wound to stop air entering and seek help immediately.

2 If there is no sucking noise, examine the wounded area and look for anything sticking out of your cat. This could be a broken branch or maybe an arrow. If there is anything protruding from your cat's chest or abdomen, again you will have to take it to the vet immediately. **Do not** attempt to remove the object.

2a Pad the area around the wound with sterile dressings.

2b Bandage around the area tightly to stop the object moving.

2c Take your cat to the veterinary surgery as carefully as possible.

3 If there is no sucking noise, and nothing is protruding from your cat's chest or abdomen, clip the hair around the wounded area to gain access.

4 Check for broken glass or other small objects around or in the wound itself. If you see any, carefully remove with tweezers. Move the skin around the wound to see if it requires stitches.

5 Flush the wound out thoroughly using clean water. Do not apply antiseptic.

6 Cover the wound with sterile dressings such as new gauze pads or other sanitary material.

7 Place your hand over the dressed area and apply pressure. If blood continues to soak through the dressing, DO NOT remove it, but add further sterile dressings. Keep applying pressure and dressings for 5 minutes. If bleeding has still not stopped, take your cat to the vet's, still applying pressure.

8 Once you have staunched the bleeding, wrap it in bandaging material (see *Principles of Bandaging*). Tape the bandages just tightly enough to keep them in place.

9 If the wound needs stitches, take your cat to the vet as soon as possible (see *Transporting Your Cat Safely*).

Bleeding Ear

As with humans, cats' ears tend to bleed profusely. Depending on the breed, cats' ears can also be quite prone to cuts, due to their inquisitive natures. Fortunately, a bleeding ear is one of the easier wounds to treat with first aid.

1 Safely restrain your cat using verbal calming techniques.

2 Taking a sterile dressing or clean cloth, fold it around the edge of your cat's ear where it is bleeding. Apply pressure on both sides of the ear with your fingers and thumb.

3 Bandage your cat's entire ear (see *Principles of Bandaging*) in this position.

4 Transport your cat to the vet for immediate attention (see *Transporting Your Cat Safely*).

Internal Bleeding

Unlike external bleeding, if your cat is bleeding internally, it requires emergency treatment whatever the circumstances. Basically, if your cat has internal bleeding, you have an emergency on your hands. Also, unlike external bleeding, you may not actually see blood. These are the signs to look for in relation to internal bleeding in your cat:

- Pale or white gums
- Rapid heartbeat and / or breathing
- Bleeding from the ears
- Bleeding from the nose
- Bleeding from the mouth
- Bleeding from the rectum

If you see any of these signs, you need to get your cat to a vet immediately. If your cat has pale or white gums, it is almost certainly in shock. To check:

- Lift your cat's lip gently to check its upper gum line. If the gum is pink, your cat is not in shock. If it is pale or white, you have an emergency.

- Put your finger tips firmly on your cat's rib cage a couple of inches from the elbow of either leg. Count the number of heartbeats in 10 seconds, and multiply by 6. If this comes to more than 150 per minute, your cat could be in shock due to internal bleeding.

After calling the vet, take the following action to treat your cat for shock:

- Lie it on its side with its nose pulled slightly upward to keep its airway clear. Gently pull your cat's tongue forward through its mouth.

- Lift your cat's rear end off the floor using a cushion, pillow, folded blanket or towels.

- Wrap your cat in a foil blanket if you have one, or other warm blanket or jacket, to conserve its body heat.

Transport your cat to the veterinary surgery immediately (see *Transporting Your Cat Safely*).

8

Treating Burns

L ike bleeding, burns are very unpleasant for your cat. Burns are also extremely painful. Your cat is likely to be worried by the smell of its own blood, but the pain of a burn will terrify it. Treating burns has to be done very carefully, and requires courage on your part, not least in coping with your cat's distress. Burns are best treated as quickly as possible, so having the skills to deal with them at your fingertips is a great bonus for all responsible cat owners.

Your cat can suffer burns from hot objects, electrical appliances or chemical substances. It will be very distressed, so you should use your verbal calming skills to start safely restraining it. If your cat has bitten through a cable, turn off the power at source and push your cat away from the cable with a non conducting object, such as a piece of wood, if you have to. Once you're sure there is no further danger from electricity, treat your cat's burn wounds if it has any.

First and Second Degree Burns

These are the less serious types of burn and are therefore easiest to treat with first aid. That does not mean they are not painful; your cat is still likely to be in some distress. Also, minor burns can be harder to spot than more serious ones, especially in cats with thick or long coats.

First degree burns can show up as singe marks, which you may be able to smell. Under the fur, your cat may have welts, very red skin and / or blisters. In second degree burns, symptoms are similar, but more pronounced. Your cat will be very distressed and may have tan coloured lesions with blisters. In either of these cases;

- To take the heat away from the burn, apply cold water. **Do not** apply ice directly, as this itself burns the skin. If it is practicable, hold the burn near a running tap or hosepipe. The flow of water should not be strong enough to damage your cat's skin, but enough to maintain a constant, cold stream.

- The sooner you apply cold water, the quicker your cat will feel its pain ease, and the less damage the burn will cause in the long term. Maintain a cold flow for at least 15 minutes. If your cat has a burnt paw, you can put it in a bucket of iced water for the same length of time, as long as there is plenty of water and not just ice.

- After 15 minutes, remove the water source and pad the wound dry. Do not wipe or rub the area, as you do not want to actually move the wounded skin. Apply gentle pressure to absorb excess water. **Do not** use cotton wool or any lint bearing material which will leave fibres on the wound.

- When the wound is dry, apply a sterile dressing. Use fresh gauze pads from your cat's first aid kid and lie them gently on the surface of the burn. DO NOT apply any creams or emollients. Wrap the dressing in bandages, not too tightly but enough to keep the dressings in place. (See *Principles of Bandaging*.)

- Take your cat to the vet as soon as possible (see *Transporting Your Cat Safely*).

Third Degree Burns

These are, obviously, the most serious types of burn, and can require many treatments. Your cat's skin may be destroyed across the burn area, or you may notice lesions which are pure black or white in colour. Your cat's fur might come away from its skin easily if it is severely burned. If your cat has third degree burns, there is also a chance that it might be suffering from shock. To check:

- Lift your cat's lip gently to check its upper gum line. If the gum pale or white, your cat is very probably suffering from shock.

- Put your finger tips firmly on your cat's rib cage a couple of inches from the elbow of either leg. Count the number of heartbeats in 10 seconds, and multiply by 6. If this comes to more than 150 per minute, your cat could be in shock.

If it is, you will have to treat this as well as the burns until you can get your cat to the veterinary surgery. Lie it on its side with its head extended. Gently pull its tongue forward through its mouth to open its airway, and lift its hind quarters off the floor slightly, supporting it with cushion or folded blanket. Use your cat's foil blanket from its first aid kit if you have one, or any blanket or jacket, to conserve its body heat.

To treat the burns themselves, the best thing you can do is protect them from further damage until your cat sees a vet.

- **Do not** apply butter or any type of ointment. Contrary to what some people might think, this actually keeps heat in the wound, causing more damage and longer suffering for your cat in the long run.

- Apply a sterile dressing to the burn, making sure to avoid cotton. Bandage the dressing gently, just enough to keep it in place.

- Take your cat to the vet immediately (see *Transporting Your Cat Safely*).

Chemical Burns

Cats sometimes suffer from burns caused by chemicals kept around the home. If you notice that your cat is in some distress and is licking a particular area, it might be because of a chemical burn. If so, you will probably be able to smell the chemical concerned; typical substances which cause burns are turpentine, insecticides or petrol.

If you detect a chemical substance on your cat's coat, apply safe restraint as necessary. Once you have control, do the following:

- Wash the affected area with soapy water. Do this thoroughly, as many times as it takes. You should be able to get all of the offending chemical off your cat's coat and skin. **Do not** be tempted to use any kind of solvent. Gentle soap and slightly warm water is perfect for the job.

- Ring the veterinary surgery and ask for any further advice. You may not have to take your cat to the vet (see *Transporting Your Cat Safely*).

Cats sometimes suffer from burns caused by chemicals kept around the home. If you notice that your cat is in some distress and is licking a particular area, it might be because of a chemical burn.

9

Heatstroke and Hypothermia

ats are susceptible to extremes of temperature in ways human beings are not. They can control their body heat in certain ways but can be vulnerable in some circumstances. As cats are curious, intelligent animals, they like to get out and explore. This sometimes means they get themselves into situations which are dangerous for them. No cat looks at the weather forecast before leaving the house, and none is likely to wonder if the water is too cold to swim in.

Heatstroke and hypothermia can overcome your cat remarkably quickly and can be extremely hazardous to their health. Fortunately, there are ways to spot if your cat is suffering from these conditions, and steps you can take to help it recover.

Heatstroke

Cats can suffer from heatstroke if they are out in direct sunlight for too long. As they tend to patrol their territory when they feel the need, they do not always consider the possible effects of the weather. Their fur is designed to keep them warm, and their ears absorb a lot of energy from the sun.

The term heatstroke refers to physical symptoms which are similar to a stroke and are caused by heat. A cat's body temperature can reach as high as 107 degrees Fahrenheit, or 41.5 Celsius. At this temperature, its internal organs are at risk of shutting down. Signs your cat may be suffering from heatstroke are:

- It drools excessively and continuously

- It loses its normal coordination

- Its breathing is extremely rapid

- The top of its head is physically hot to the touch.

If you notice one or more of these symptoms, and your cat has been in a hot environment for any length of time, you should act quickly. The sooner you cool your cat down, the more chance it has of making a recovery.

Essential Steps

The first thing to do is to remove your cat from the source of the heat. If you have left it in your car, carry it out to somewhere cool, or at least in the shade outside your vehicle. If you have a larger breed of cat, you may need help; but on no account leave your cat where it is. If you are out in the sun, take your cat to a shaded are quickly.

1 As soon as you can, get your cat to a place which has cold water and some ice:

2 Cool your cat down by running a cold garden hose over it. If you can, run a cold bath at the same time. Hose your cat down in cold water and / or place in a cold bath for at least half an hour. The heat from its body will take this long to disperse through its skin and coat.

3 If you have ice, apply ice packs directly to the top of your cat's head, in between its ears. Coats are usually quite thin at that point, and blood vessels run close to the surface.

4 Keep applying ice packs continuously until you hand your cat over to the vet (see *Transporting Your Cat Safely*).

> If you have ice, apply ice packs directly to the top of your cat's head, in between its ears. Coats are usually quite thin at that point, and blood vessels run close to the surface.

Hypothermia

At the other end of the scale, hypothermia is when a body's core temperature falls below a certain level. This can happen when a cat is exposed to freezing air conditions, or simply falls in or swims in very cold water. As water temperatures in the sea and rivers are often much colder than people think, this is quite easily done. Once your cat's fur is soaked, it has no insulation qualities, and the cold of the water directly affects the blood and internal organs.

The term hypothermia literally means not enough heat. Cats usually have quite high body temperatures, at about 100 to 101 degrees Fahrenheit, or 38 degrees Celsius. If this falls to below 90 Fahrenheit or 32 Celsius, it can have serious consequences. These are the signs to look for if you think your cat may be suffering from hypothermia:

● Depression. This might sound strange, but hypothermia makes cats feel depressed and lethargic. You will be able to spot this very easily, especially if your cat is usually active and inquisitive.

● Shivering spells. Hypothermia produces shivering spells, which stop as suddenly as they start.

● Dilated pupils. If your cat's eyes have especially large pupils for the light conditions, it may have hypothermia.

● Your cat might actually feel cold to the touch, on its skin or coat.

If you think your cat has hypothermia, you need to warm it up before taking it to the vet. The best way to do this is with a hot water bottle, placed next to your cat's abdomen.

- Wrap the water bottle in cloth or a towel to avoid it burning the skin.
- Wrap your cat in a blanket or jacket
- Take it to the vet immediately (see *Transporting Your Cat Safely*).

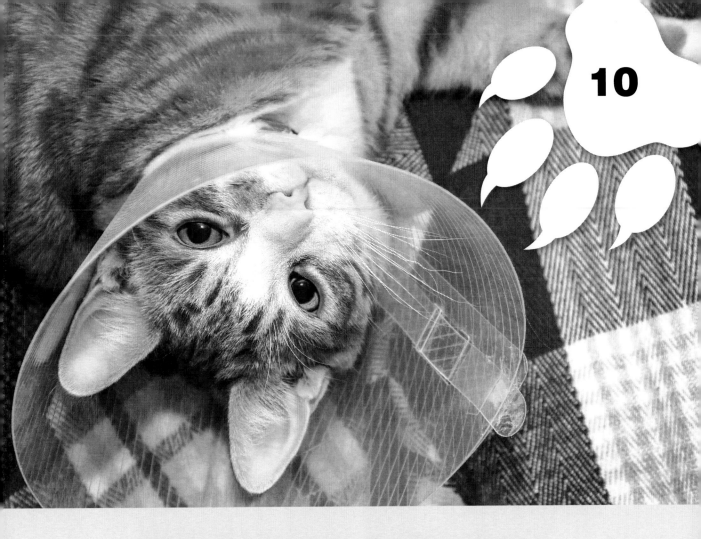

10

Common Injuries and Illnesses

There are a number of ways in which your cat can suddenly feel ill, or types of injury which most cats get regularly. The more experience you have of each of these, the easier you will be able to deal with them. Not all require a visit to the vet, so you can have your cat up and running again as soon as possible. Others are more serious, but, as we have seen with some quite challenging scenarios, the right first aid is a fantastic way of giving your cat the best chance of recovery.

Any cat owner will have to face a number of challenges, especially over the many years of a cat's lifetime. Some of the illnesses and injuries which befall them might sound unlikely, but in fact these are the type of things faced by cat owners all the time. If any of them happens to your cat, don't worry; it's nothing that millions of owners haven't faced before.

Urinary Tract Infections (UTIs)

One of the things which affects cats more than any other common ailment is Urinary Tract Infection. While other types of pets have their own associated disease risks, UTI is the one usually associated with cats. In fact, it is usually mature, male cats which suffer from urinary tract infections, although mature females do too.

The cause of the disease is the design of your cat's anatomy, specifically its urethra. This is the channel through which your pet's waste products pass from its kidneys to the point of release. These products are called urine, and the channel the urethra, or Urinary Tract (UT).

Due to evolution, male cats have a narrower urethra than female cats. This makes any infection of the urinary tract more likely, and those infections more serious. Bacteria find it easy to lodge in the urethra, and quickly spread backwards into your cat's body. This causes a change in the acidity of the urine, which leads in turn to the formation of crystals.

If a cat's urethra becomes blocked completely, this will be fatal unless treated promptly.

> While other types of pets have their own associated disease risks, UTI is the one usually associated with cats.

Symptoms

Problems with urination are only one of the signs of a possible UTI. Here is a more complete list:

- Straining when urinating
- Blood in the urine

- Crying when urinating
- Urinating in unusual places
- Licking the urinary area
- Depression
- Lack of appetite.
- Lethargy.

Some of these symptoms may indicate other diseases. However, in conjunction with others, they might help you spot the onset of a UTI. Remember, these infections are especially common in mature and male cats.

Prevention

The very best method of first aid is to prevent the illness or injury happening in the first place. You can reduce your pet's chances of contracting a UTI by

- Use a low pH litter. This will turn blue when your cat's urine shows any sign of infection.
- Keep your cat's litter tray clean at all times, to stop bacteria spreading
- Feed your cat properly, so it doesn't become overweight and / or diabetic. These conditions increase the chance of your cat developing UTIs.
- Keep your cat happy. Stress is a recognised contributory factor to cats acquiring UTIs.

Treatment

Unfortunately, the only cure for UTIs is prevention. If your cat develops a severe infection, you must take it to the vet immediately (see Transporting Your Cat Safely).

Seizures

Convulsions, or seizures as they are also known, can be worrying, as they often seem to come out of nowhere. Your cat may never have one, but if it does, try to remember that cats have seizures all the time, for a number of reasons. Facing your first one will be the hardest.

It may help you to know what a convulsion actually is. It happens when your cat's brain sends a stream of electrical signals to its muscles, in an unusual pattern. All muscles work in response to these signals, but with a convulsion there are too many signals for the muscles to cope with. What happens is that the muscle tissue locks, much like a computer when it is trying to respond to too many commands.

Once your cat's muscles have locked, they will take time to recover their normal functions. This is what happens in the vast majority of cases; there is no permanent damage. In the meantime, of course, watching your cat have a seizure is not pleasant.

Epilepsy is one cause of seizures, but by no means the only one. Other causes of seizures are:

- Poisoning by lead or other substances
- Liver diseases
- Kidney failure
- Brain tumour

Obviously, you don't want your cat to be suffering from any of the above. While seizures are common, their causes need to be ascertained as quickly as possible. Any time your cat has a seizure, make sure you take it to the veterinary surgery as soon as possible afterwards.

Seizures usually last a few minutes, after which your cat will be confused and possibly a bit dazed. This will last for between 15 minutes and half an hour. While the seizure itself is actually happening, the biggest risks to your cat's health come from it injuring itself. As it has no control over its muscles, you have to take steps to keep your cat safe.

The most important thing to remember is not to panic. The seizure will stop of its own accord, and you will just have to be patient until it does. In the meantime, these are the essential steps to take:

Carefully take hold of your cat by whatever parts of its body give you best purchase, ideally its lower legs. Pull it away from any walls or large objects such as furniture, so it doesn't injure itself.

Wrap your cat in a blanket or towel to give it extra protection against injury.

If the seizure lasts for more than 10 minutes, or if your cat has another seizure within an hour, it needs to go to the vet.

Once your cat comes out of its seizure, call your vet while it is recovering. They will give you any further instructions they think appropriate based on what you tell them.

Take your cat to the veterinary surgery. (See our section on *Transporting Your Cat Safely*.)

Stings and Foreign Bodies

Stings

Your cat could suffer from a sting at any time. This can happen as easily in the home as when out and about in the city or the countryside. As with humans, cats can suffer allergic reactions to stings. If this happens, you need to get your cat to a veterinary surgery as soon as possible. In the meantime, here are some steps you can take to help your cat through the worst of an allergic reaction to a sting:

- If you notice any local swelling (also called urticaria) on your cat's face, paw or leg, this could be the sign of a sting. If you can see a sting in your cat's skin, remove it with tweezers, or your fingers if you can.

- Call the vet and ask their advice. It could be that giving your cat a Piriton tablet is all that it needs. Be sure to ask for advice first, however.

- If your cat has been stung by a bee, after removing the sting itself, treat the wounded area with a solution of sodium bicarbonate.

- If your cat has been stung by a wasp, rub the area with apple cider vinegar if you have any. The compounds in this vinegar help neutralise the venom in the wasp sting.

- If the sting is on your cat's face or throat area, you need to call a vet quickly. Short nosed cats especially are vulnerable to facial stings. Take your cat to the vet as soon as possible (see the section on *Transporting Your Cat Safely*).

Foreign Bodies

If your cat gets some kind of foreign body in its eye, it will become distressed. If you notice any distress, and see your cat trying to paw its eye or shake its head violently, it could be trying to rid itself of the object or creature. As they eye is a very sensitive area, these can be painful and worrying for your cat.

Safely restrain your cat and examine its eyes. If you see a foreign body in either of them, try to remove it. The best way to do this is with slightly salty water but tap or bottled water will do. Gently try to remove the object by flushing your cat's eye.

If the foreign body has actually penetrated your cat's eye, this is an emergency. **Do not** try to remove the object or creature but call your vet immediately and try to pacify your cat as much as possible.

Of course, the best course of action after any foreign body ingestion is to take your cat to the vet immediately. See the section on *Transporting Your Cat Safely*.

Animal Bites

As a lively, inquisitive and intuitive animal, your cat will inevitably encounter other animals on its travels. As well as other cats, there are plenty of other species roaming round our countryside and cities. As many of these are carnivores, they all have sharp teeth which can give very nasty bites. These are very easy to pick up, and can happen in the blink of an eye.

Checking Wounds

If your cat has been involved in a fight, it's important you check for any wounds. Some of these may be obvious, but your pet may have a number of hidden wounds under its fur. Tooth puncture wounds are common around the neck area, and on the legs. After safely restraining your cat, check its coat for any signs of blood.

After any fight with another animal, but especially a wild one, it's important to think about **Rabies**. Your cat will have been inoculated against this, but others may not have been. If you are not sure of the status of your cat's rabies inoculation, check with your vet immediately. If the other animal is a family pet, find out from its owner the status of its rabies inoculation; however, in the case of a wild animal, strict procedures should be followed.

The only way to check if a wild animal has rabies is for it to be destroyed and have its brain examined by a vet. How you go about this will vary according to circumstances but remember never to touch a wild animal with your bare hands, even if it's dead. If it is, you'll need to wear gloves and use a blanket to take the animal to the vet for examination.

Bite Treatments

If your cat has been bitten, these are the steps you should take:

- Apply safe restraint and immobilising your cat's head. Bite wounds are very painful, and your cat may try to bite you.

- Clip your cat's hair around the bite wound area. Flush the wound thoroughly with clean water, and DO NOT use any domestic antiseptics, as these will be very painful on bite wounds.

- Inspect the wound carefully. Use your fingertips to move the skin gently around the bite, to see if the teeth marks are deep enough to require stitches, or your cat's flesh is torn.

- If the wound stops bleeding, DO NOT apply dressings or bandages. It should be left to drain of its own accord.

- If it continues to bleed, try to staunch the bleeding. Put a sterile dressing over the wound and press down hard. If bleeding continues, add another dressing and repeat until bleeding stops.

If you think the wound requires stitches, take your cat to the veterinary surgery immediately (see our section on *Transporting Your Cat Safely*).

Poisoning

While it might sound dramatic, poisoning is something that happens to cats rather a lot. Unlike with humans, where this is the result of some terrible plot, cats often poison themselves accidentally. Taking poison basically means eating or drinking something you shouldn't or which is bad for you. Cats eat and drink an awful lot of things they probably shouldn't. While you can try to keep your cat away from harmful substances, its natural curiosity and extremely sensitive nose will take it to places you just can't control.

This can happen at any time. There could be poisonous material of any sort hidden in the grass or under leaves. Unfortunately, sometimes the only way you and your cat find out if they are poisonous is after your cat has tried to eat or drink them.

This might happen second hand, or paw, as it were. If your cat steps in something, its nature will be to lick itself clean. It could be carrying round liquids or solids on its paws while out on its rounds, and not lick the substance off until it gets home.

Substances Poisonous to cats

Cats can be poisoned by an amazing amount of substances. Unfortunately, a lot of these are kept around the average home. Try to keep your cat away from the following:

- Anything alcoholic
- ammonia
- antifreeze
- bleach
- chocolate (especially baking chocolate)
- detergent
- disinfectant
- dry-cleaning solution
- fertiliser
- furniture polish
- glue
- grapes and raisins
- human medication
- mothballs
- mouse and rat poison
- onions
- oven cleaner
- paint thinner and remover
- petrol
- shoe polish
- silver polish
- toilet bowl cleaner.

If that weren't enough to worry about, many household plants are poisonous to cats. These include:

- Aloe Vera
- amaryllis
- avocado
- azalea
- bird of paradise
- calla lily
- castor bean
- corn plant
- cyclamen
- daffodil
- day lily
- dieffenbachia
- Easter lily
- elephant ears
- English ivy
- gladiolus
- holly
- hyacinth
- hydrangea
- iris
- kalanchoe
- macadamia nut
- mistletoe
- narcissus
- philodendron
- poinsettia
- rhododendron
- tomato plant
- tulip
- yew
- yucca.

Signs of Poisoning

Signs to look for if your cat has been poisoned are:

- Excessive drooling
- Seizures
- Coma
- Vomiting

- Diarrhoea
- Abdominal pain
- Twitching
- Nervousness

- Chemical smell somewhere on the body.

If your cat falls into a coma or has a seizure after obviously ingesting a poisonous substance, it is best to stay on the safe side and take it to the vet straight away, along with the substance it has ingested. Wrap your cat in a blanket and take it to the veterinary surgery (see the section on *Transporting Your Cat Safely*).

If you detect a chemical smell anywhere on your cat, you should wash it completely. Use warm, soapy water and bathe or clean your cat's entire coat several times until the smell has completely gone. You may also like to flush out your cat's mouth with clean water in case it has licked itself. Keep an eye out for any signs of poisoning.

You may need to make your cat vomit. This is not always advisable, however. If your cat has ingested any caustic or petroleum based products, **do not** force it to vomit. Caustic substances include battery acid, corn and callous remover, dish washing detergent, drain cleaner, grease remover, lye, and oven cleaner. Petroleum based products include paint solvent, floor wax, and dry-cleaning solution.

If your cat has not already vomited, and you are sure it has not ingested any caustic or petroleum based product, you should induce it to vomit. To do this safely:

Based on your cat's weight, give it one tablespoon of hydrogen peroxide per 20 pounds of weight. Do this every ten minutes until your cat starts to vomit. If it has not vomited after half an hour, take your cat to the veterinary surgery immediately (see the section on *Transporting Your Cat Safely*).

If you suspect your cat may have ingested anything poisonous, contact your local Veterinary Practitioner or Animal Welfare Office.

Final Word

We hope you have found this guide to first aid for your cat helpful. For most of your cat's life, you won't have to try to help it. With its home comforts and room to roam, your cat should stay healthy and happy. As we have seen, however, cats do have a habit of getting into fights and chasing, disabling, biting and eating things they shouldn't. This is perfectly natural behaviour, and you wouldn't want it any other way. The point is to look for warning signs they will try to hide from you.

Some elements of first aid discussed here should be part of your routine with your cat. Administering medication, for example, is something which every cat has to get used to, however much they hate it. Of course, the more you practice, the better you get at it. This will probably mean giving them things that are good for them without them knowing; probably by disguising them in things your cat loves eating.

Other first aid techniques in this guide are for everyday occurrences. As we have seen, even finding out about fights is not easy. Any war wounds are, however, usually minor, and can be dealt with properly if you spot them early enough.

While many of these do not require veterinary attention, some are best followed up in this way, just for your own peace of mind. If so, learning how to transport your cat safely is an excellent set of skills to have. However healthy your cat is, it will have to visit the veterinary surgery every now and then, so making the process as painless as possible can only be a good thing.

Some techniques in this guide are for really quite serious injuries and illnesses. As we hope we have shown, you can take control of almost any situation. If you need to attend courses to give you confidence, by all means do so. As a responsible cat owner, the more strings you have to your bow, the better. Gaining confidence in first aid techniques can help your cat enjoy a long, happy and healthy life.